MANATEE

Amazing Facts About Nature's Gentle Giants for Kids

Dylanna Press

Meet the Manatee

SPLASH! A massive, gray shape glides silently through the crystal-clear waters of a Florida spring. Its whiskered snout breaks the surface for a breath, then sinks again as it munches on underwater grasses. You've just spotted one of the ocean's most beloved gentle giants: the West Indian manatee!

Manatees are large, peaceful marine mammals that spend their lives in warm, shallow waters. They glide through coastal rivers, springs, and lagoons from Florida to the Caribbean, following the warmth and feasting on underwater plants. These peaceful animals can weigh up to 3,500 pounds but move through water with surprising grace.

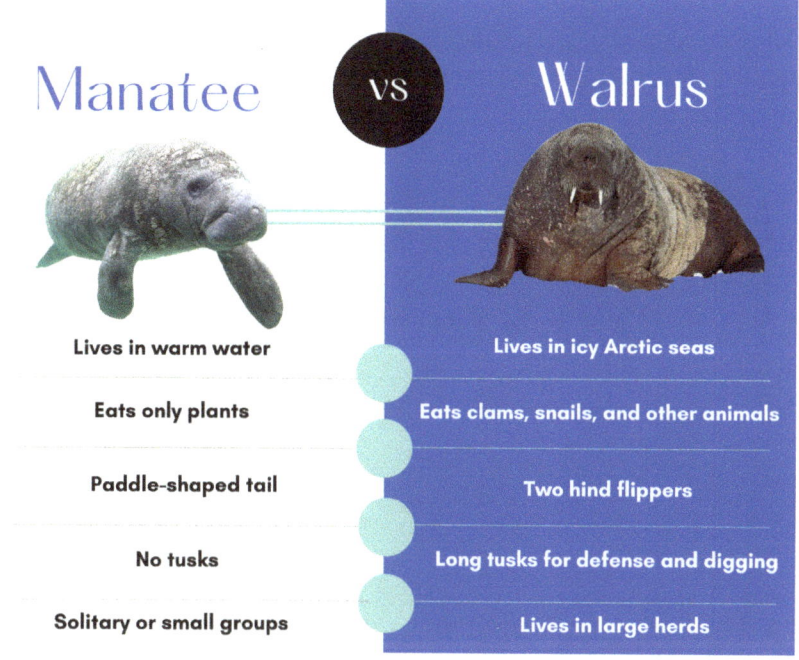

Manatee	vs	Walrus
Lives in warm water		Lives in icy Arctic seas
Eats only plants		Eats clams, snails, and other animals
Paddle-shaped tail		Two hind flippers
No tusks		Long tusks for defense and digging
Solitary or small groups		Lives in large herds

The West Indian manatee (*Trichechus manatus*), especially the Florida subspecies, is the best-known. You can find them in Florida year-round, gathering in warm-water springs in winter and exploring rivers and bays the rest of the year. They've even been seen as far south as Brazil and as far west as Texas.

What makes manatees so special? They're gentle underwater gardeners, caring mothers, and amazing travelers. They can hold their breath for 20 minutes, use their lips like fingers, and cruise for hundreds of miles in search of warm water.

Nicknamed "sea cows," manatees were once mistaken for mermaids by sailors. While not magical, these calm, whiskered animals have a charm all their own.

Manatees belong to an ancient group of mammals called Sirenia, named after mythical sirens. With no natural predators, they spend their days eating, resting, and socializing in calm coastal waters.

Once in danger from boat strikes and habitat loss, manatees are now a conservation success story. Thousands of them thrive in Florida's waterways today—delighting visitors and helping keep underwater ecosystems healthy.

What Do Manatees Look Like?

Manatees are some of the most impressive gentle giants in the aquatic world. Adults typically grow 8 to 13 feet (2.4 to 4 meters) long and weigh between 800 to 3,500 pounds (360 to 1,600 kg). That's roughly the size and weight of a small SUV! Females are usually larger than males, which helps them carry and nurse their babies.

The most striking feature of a manatee is its massive, torpedo-shaped body perfectly designed for gliding through water. Their thick, wrinkled gray skin feels like a wet basketball and helps them stay warm in cooler water. Unlike sleek dolphins that zip through the ocean, manatees are built for slow, steady, peaceful swimming.

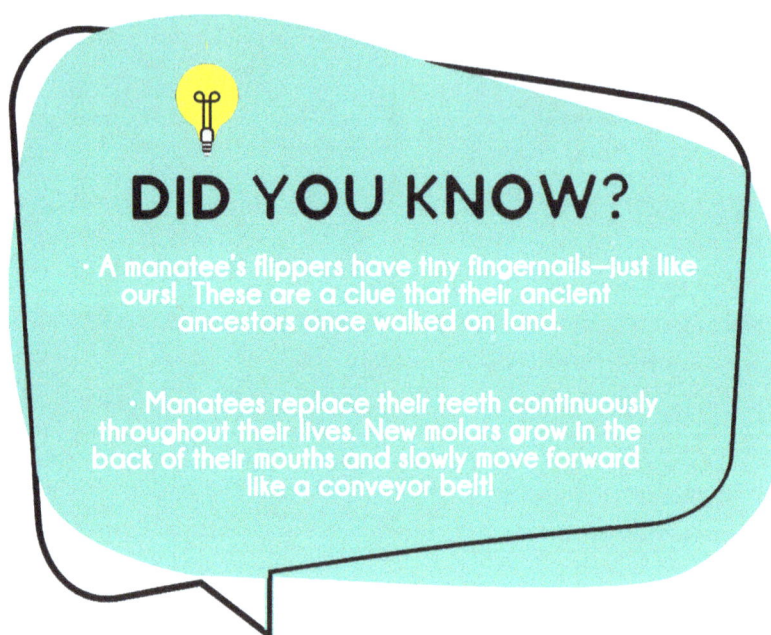

DID YOU KNOW?

• A manatee's flippers have tiny fingernails—just like ours! These are a clue that their ancient ancestors once walked on land.

• Manatees replace their teeth continuously throughout their lives. New molars grow in the back of their mouths and slowly move forward like a conveyor belt!

Their broad, paddle-shaped flippers and large, rounded tail fluke are among their most distinctive features. The flippers, which evolved from legs, even have tiny fingernails—reminders of their ancient land-dwelling ancestors. Manatees use these flexible limbs to steer, "walk" along the bottom, and even embrace one another in gentle underwater hugs.

Perhaps their most endearing trait is their face. With small, kind-looking eyes and nostrils perched on top of their snout, manatees can breathe easily while most of their body stays underwater. Their star feature? A split upper lip bristling with thousands of sensitive whiskers, called vibrissae. It works like a combination nose, hand, and food scoop—grabbing and guiding plants right into their mouths.

Although they don't have visible ears, manatees hear well—especially low-frequency sounds, which helps them avoid danger from passing boats.

Their broad tail fluke powers their slow, graceful swimming. Unlike fish, which swish side to side, manatees move their tails up and down, like whales. With each slow-motion beat of that powerful tail, these massive mammals drift peacefully through their underwater world.

Where Do Manatees Live?

West Indian manatees are citizens of warm, shallow waters throughout the western Atlantic Ocean and Caribbean Sea. These gentle giants inhabit coastal areas from Florida and the Gulf of Mexico all the way south to Brazil, always seeking the perfect mix of warmth, food, and peace.

Florida manatees have the most well-studied range. In warmer months, they fan out across the entire Florida coastline and sometimes travel as far north as the Carolinas or as far west as Louisiana. A few bold travelers have even been spotted in the Chesapeake Bay—and once near New York!

DID YOU KNOW?

- Manatees are like aquatic snowbirds—they migrate to warm-water refuges in winter and spread out to feeding areas in summer.
- Florida's Crystal River is home to the largest gathering of manatees in the world during winter months.
- Some manatees return to the exact same warm-water spots year after year, like visiting favorite vacation destinations.

But when the water temperature drops below 68°F (20°C), manatees go on the move. Like living thermometers, they head straight for warm-water refuges. Natural springs, power plant discharge areas, and deep rivers become seasonal manatee gathering spots. Places like Crystal River, Blue Spring State Park, and the warm-water zones near power plants turn into bustling manatee cities each winter.

Manatees prefer shallow water—usually less than 20 feet (6 meters) deep—where they can surface easily to breathe and graze on seagrass beds. They love calm, quiet places where freshwater rivers meet the sea, including coastal lagoons, canals, and estuaries.

Even though they live in saltwater, manatees need access to fresh water for drinking. They often visit springs, rivers, or even marina docks where people rinse boats. Some curious manatees have even been caught sipping from hoses or dripping water spigots!

Caribbean manatees live in similar habitats throughout the greater Caribbean, from Puerto Rico and the Virgin Islands down to Venezuela and Brazil. While they face many of the same challenges as Florida manatees, they often receive less protection and are more difficult to monitor.

Super Survivors – Manatee Adaptations

Manatees are perfectly engineered for their peaceful, plant-eating lifestyle in warm, shallow waters. Every part of their massive body tells the story of millions of years of evolution as gentle aquatic herbivores.

- **Breathing Champions** – Manatees can hold their breath for 15 to 20 minutes while resting, though they usually surface every 2 to 5 minutes. When they do breathe, they can replace up to 90% of the air in their lungs in just one breath—much more efficient than humans! Their nostrils have special valves that seal tight underwater.

- **Amazing Lips** – A manatee's split upper lip is one of nature's most incredible tools. Covered in thousands of sensitive whiskers, these flexible lips can move independently like two separate hands. They can feel textures, taste plants, grab food, and sort through vegetation with amazing precision—all while determining which plants are the most nutritious!

- **Dense Bones** – Unlike most marine mammals that have lightweight bones for floating, manatees have solid, heavy bones that help them sink. This adaptation allows them to "walk" along the bottom and stay comfortably submerged while munching on bottom-growing seagrass.

- **Temperature Detectors** – Manatees are incredibly sensitive to water temperature changes and will travel hundreds of miles to find water that's just right. They're like living thermometers, always seeking that perfect 72°F (22°C) comfort zone.

- **Incredible Digestion** – Manatees have one of the longest digestive systems in the animal kingdom—over 130 feet (40 meters) long! This gives their bodies plenty of time to extract every bit of nutrition from tough, low-energy plants.

- **Buoyancy Masters** – By adjusting the air in their lungs, manatees can control whether they float, hover in the water column, or rest peacefully on the bottom. They're like living submarines with perfect depth control.

- **Slow and Steady** – Manatees have an extremely slow metabolism, which means they don't need as much food or energy as other animals their size. This efficiency helps them thrive on a diet of relatively low-nutrition plants.

These adaptations make manatees perfectly suited for their role as the ocean's gardeners.

What Do Manatees Eat?

Manatees are nature's ultimate vegetarians, and they take their plant-eating job very seriously! These aquatic herbivores spend 6 to 8 hours each day grazing on aquatic plants, consuming around 4 to 9% of their body weight daily. For a 2,000-pound manatee, that adds up to 80 to 180 pounds of food every day!

Their absolute favorite foods are seagrasses—underwater meadows that grow in sandy or muddy bottoms along the coast. Turtle grass, manatee grass (yes, it's really named after them!), shoal grass, and widgeon grass top their preferred menu. These nutritious plants offer just the right blend of vitamins and minerals to keep manatees healthy and strong.

Manatees are like gentle underwater lawn mowers. Using their split lips, they grab plants and carefully tear them free from the seafloor. They don't have front teeth for cutting, so those lips do all the work. Inside their mouth, they have flat back teeth that work like a conveyor belt—as front teeth wear down from constant chewing, new ones move forward from the back. A manatee can go through hundreds or even thousands of teeth in its lifetime!

MANATEE MATH

> 1. If a manatee eats 250 pounds of plants per day, how many pounds does it eat in one week?
>
> 2. A manatee spends 8 hours a day eating. How many minutes is that?

A: 1,750 POUNDS PER WEEK; 480 MINUTES PER DAY

In freshwater areas, manatees diversify their diet by munching on floating plants like water hyacinth, water lettuce, and pickerelweed. They've been observed eating more than 60 different plant species—and occasionally scraping algae off rocks, docks, or boats.

What's especially fascinating is how gently manatees feed. They rarely disturb plant roots, allowing seagrass beds to regrow quickly after grazing. As they feed, they leave behind narrow "feeding trails"—clear paths through the vegetation that scientists can spot from above to track where manatees have been.

By keeping seagrass meadows trimmed and healthy, manatees play the role of underwater gardeners. Their grazing promotes new growth, prevents overgrowth, and creates ideal habitat for fish, crabs, and countless other marine creatures.

Social Giants

Despite their massive size, manatees are gentle, social animals with interesting relationships and ways of communicating. While they don't form permanent pods like dolphins, they regularly gather in loose groups and interact in ways that reveal their peaceful, intelligent nature.

Manatees often come together in aggregations, especially during winter when they crowd into warm-water refuges. These gatherings can include just a few individuals or hundreds of manatees floating, resting, and socializing together like a calm underwater community.

The strongest bond is between mothers and their calves. Baby manatees stay with their mothers for 1 to 2 years, learning essential survival skills like where to find the best plants, how to locate warm water, and how to avoid danger. During this time, mother and calf communicate constantly and are rarely separated.

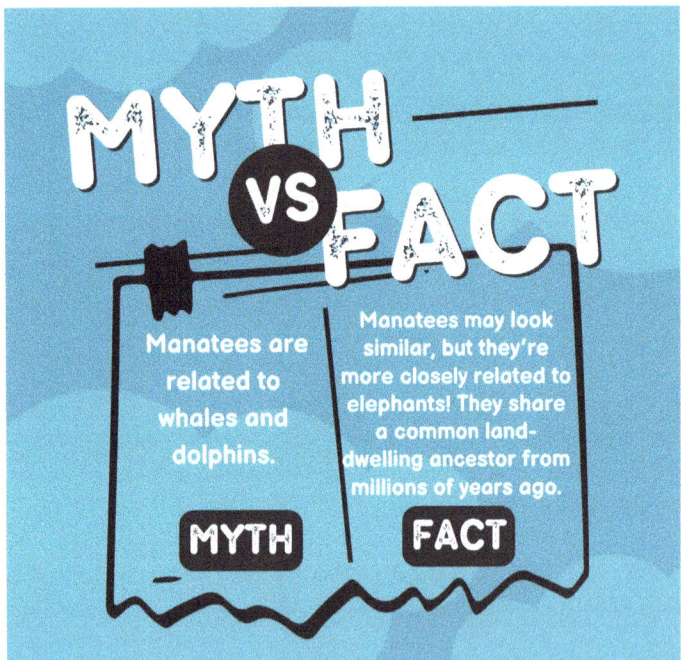

Manatees are more vocal than you might expect! They make squeaks, chirps, whistles, and chirping sounds that travel through the water like underwater bird songs. These sounds help them stay in touch, especially in crowded environments. Each manatee has its own voice, and mother-calf pairs can recognize each other's calls even in a group.

Touch is also a key part of manatee communication. They nuzzle, bump, and even hug each other with their flippers. Playful young manatees engage in games of chase, slow-motion wrestling, and follow-the-leader. Adults often rest close together in peaceful groups—sometimes even stacked like gentle underwater pancakes.

When encountering something new, such as a snorkeler or camera, manatees approach slowly and curiously. With flippers outstretched like an underwater handshake, they explore using their sensitive lips—always calm, always kind.

During mating season, groups of male manatees form what scientists call a "mating herd." They follow a female for days at a time, competing patiently and gently for her attention. These gatherings highlight the peaceful nature of manatee interactions—even in competition.

On the Move

Manatees are among nature's most determined temperature seekers, traveling hundreds of miles in their endless quest for warm water. Unlike most animals that migrate for food or breeding, manatees migrate for one simple reason: to stay warm.

These animals are surprisingly mobile despite their peaceful, slow-motion lifestyle. During warm months, Florida manatees spread out along the entire southeastern coast, traveling as far north as Virginia and as far west as Texas. Individual manatees have been tracked making journeys of over 1,000 miles (1,600 km) in a single season!

Their superpower? Temperature sensitivity. Manatees can detect changes in water temperature as small as 1 or 2 degrees. When water dips below 68°F (20°C), it triggers their instinct to move toward warmer waters, especially around the 72°F (22°C) comfort zone they prefer.

These migrations aren't random. Manatees often follow the same travel routes year after year, returning to favorite warm-water refuges like Crystal River and Blue Spring State Park. Scientists believe mothers pass this knowledge to their calves, creating generations of manatees that share the same seasonal paths.

Manatees typically cruise at a relaxed 3 to 5 miles per hour (5 to 8 km/h), but they're capable of short bursts up to 15 mph (24 km/h) when necessary. They navigate by following coastlines, underwater contours, and even scent trails created by other manatees.

During their travels, manatees communicate with others through various signs. They create "scent trails" by releasing pheromones, and they often follow the same underwater pathways, creating worn travel routes through seagrass beds and along river channels.

As climate change alters temperature patterns, traditional warm-water havens are becoming less predictable. Some manatees now travel farther or arrive earlier than before, adapting to shifting conditions—but these changes also pose new survival challenges.

pheromones – chemical signals animals use to communicate

A Day in the Life

A manatee's day is the perfect example of living life in the slow lane. These gentle giants divide their time between just a few relaxing activities: eating, resting, traveling slowly, and socializing.

Manatees don't follow strict schedules like people do. They're active both day and night but tend to do most of their feeding during daylight when visibility is best. A typical day starts whenever the manatee stirs—either from resting on the bottom or floating gently at the surface.

Even while sleeping, they must rise to breathe every few minutes. Scientists believe manatees can rest with one half of their brain at a time, similar to dolphins. This unique ability allows them to surface and breathe automatically—even mid-nap!

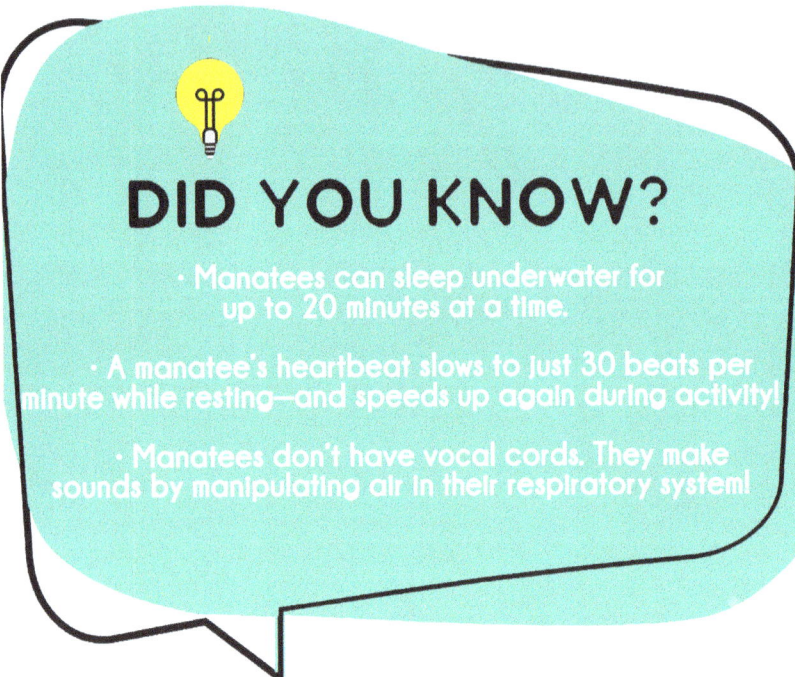

DID YOU KNOW?
- Manatees can sleep underwater for up to 20 minutes at a time.
- A manatee's heartbeat slows to just 30 beats per minute while resting—and speeds up again during activity!
- Manatees don't have vocal cords. They make sounds by manipulating air in their respiratory system!

Their mornings usually begin with a slow ascent for fresh air, followed by a visit to their favorite underwater salad bars: seagrass beds or freshwater plant areas. Feeding is unhurried and peaceful. There's no competition, no predators, and no plants trying to escape—just calm, mindful munching.

During the warmest part of the day, manatees often seek out perfectly temperate waters. They may bask in sunny, shallow areas or rest near warm springs or power plant outflows. Some float near the surface with their backs exposed to the sun, enjoying a warm soak.

Socializing happens naturally throughout the day. Manatees might meet up during feeding, rest together in a warm cove, or gently interact. Calves are especially playful, while adults enjoy the company of others in quiet, unhurried ways.

Travel occurs as needed. Manatees move between feeding spots, search for warmer water, or simply explore new territory. They're never in a hurry—every swim is taken at a relaxed pace, always with a sense of curiosity and calm.

Mating and Birth

Manatee romance is as gentle and peaceful as everything else these animals do. Unlike many animals with specific breeding seasons, manatees can mate year-round, though births are most common during warmer months when conditions are ideal for raising babies.

When a female manatee is ready to mate, she attracts the attention of several males, forming what scientists call a "mating herd." These groups can include 2 to 20 male manatees, all following one female for days or even weeks. Remarkably, this process is calm and non-aggressive. Males compete through patience, persistence, and gentle courtship behaviors rather than fighting.

During this slow-moving ritual, the group drifts together through the water. Males take turns approaching the female, using soft vocalizations, flipper touches, and close swimming to communicate interest. The female ultimately chooses a mate, and once mating occurs, the group disperses peacefully.

MYTH VS FACT

Manatees give birth on land like seals. — **MYTH**

Manatees are fully aquatic and give birth underwater. Their calves can swim and surface for air within seconds of being born. — **FACT**

After a year-long pregnancy, the mother gives birth to a single calf in a quiet, warm, shallow area—like a spring, lagoon, or calm river bend. Twins are extremely rare. These peaceful birthing areas offer newborns protection during their most vulnerable early days.

A newborn manatee is about 3 to 4 feet (1 meter) long and weighs 60 to 70 pounds (27 to 32 kg)—about the size of a large dog. Calves can swim immediately and instinctively surface for air within moments of birth. Within hours, they begin following their mothers and learning the basics of manatee life.

The bond between mother and calf is strong. Baby manatees stay close to their mother's side, often swimming just beneath her belly or holding onto her flipper with their own tiny flippers. This close contact provides comfort, protection, and constant learning opportunities.

Manatee mothers are attentive and nurturing. They nurse their calves with rich milk for the first several months and gradually introduce them to solid foods. By modeling behaviors like grazing and navigating warm-water routes, they pass along the knowledge young manatees need to survive.

Growing Up Manatee

Baby manatees are among the most adorable animals in the ocean, and they have a lot to learn during their first few years of life. Growing up as a manatee means mastering the gentle art of underwater living while staying safe and learning the skills needed for independent life.

For the first few weeks, a manatee calf depends entirely on its mother's rich, creamy milk. Manatee milk is packed with nutrients, helping babies grow quickly during this crucial early period. Calves nurse by grasping one of their mother's two nipples, located beneath her flippers. This lets them feed while easily surfacing for air.

Around 3 to 4 weeks old, calves begin experimenting with plants, though they continue nursing for several more months. Learning what to eat is essential—mothers guide them to different types of seagrass and aquatic plants, showing which ones are safe, tasty, and nutritious. Young manatees are curious and will sometimes try to nibble algae, floating debris, or even boat decorations!

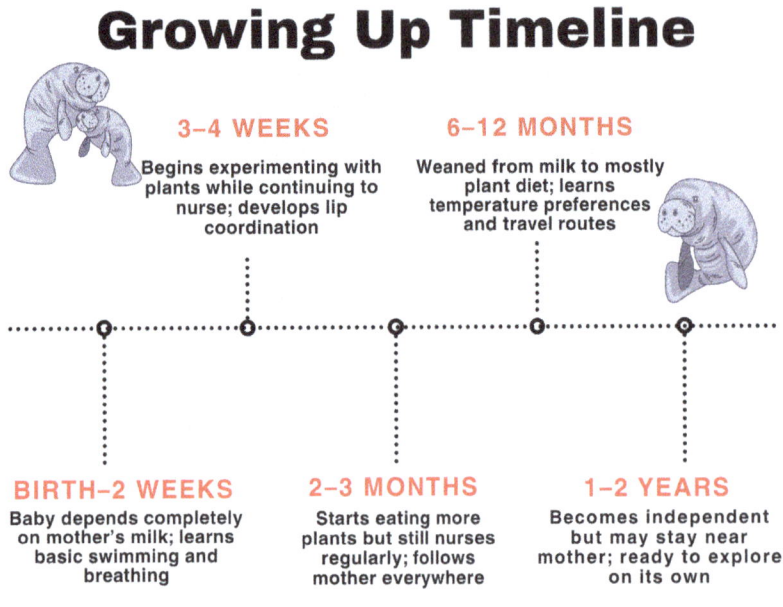

The calf's flexible lips and sensitive whiskers develop quickly. Soon, they're using them just like mom to grab, sort, and explore their food.

Watching a baby manatee learn to use its lips is like watching a human baby learn to use its hands—lots of clumsy tries followed by rapid improvement.

Swimming skills also evolve over time. Calves can swim at birth, but must learn to dive, hold their breath longer, and navigate currents. Young manatees are naturally more buoyant than adults and tend to pop to the surface like corks until they master depth control.

Social play is another key part of development. Young manatees are playful by nature—they interact with other calves, explore new objects, and engage in gentle games that help them build social confidence and communication skills.

The mother-calf bond, which typically lasts 1 to 2 years, is one of the longest parent-child relationships among marine mammals. During this time, calves learn everything from where to find food and warm water to how to safely navigate around boats and behave around other manatees—and even curious humans.

Manatees and Their Ecosystem

Manatees are much more than gentle, lovable sea cows—they're essential ecosystem engineers that help maintain the health and balance of aquatic environments throughout their range. These peaceful animals connect land and sea in ways that support countless other species and keep underwater habitats thriving.

Underwater Gardeners: Manatees are nature's perfect lawn care service! As they graze on seagrass beds, they help maintain these underwater meadows in several important ways. Their gentle feeding trims seagrass like mowing a lawn, preventing beds from becoming overgrown and allowing sunlight to reach younger plants. This "pruning" actually stimulates new growth and keeps seagrass beds healthy and productive.

Nutrient Distributors: As manatees travel between different feeding areas, they transport nutrients through their waste. They might eat plants in one location and deposit natural fertilizer somewhere else entirely, helping spread nutrients throughout the ecosystem and supporting plant growth across their range.

Habitat Creators: Large manatees create trails and clearings through dense aquatic vegetation as they move and feed. These pathways provide swimming routes for fish and other marine animals, improve water circulation, and prevent vegetation from becoming stagnant.

Indicator Species: Manatees are highly sensitive to water quality, food availability, and temperature. When manatees are thriving, it's usually a good sign the ecosystem is in balance. But when they struggle, it can be a warning that something is wrong in the broader environment.

Tourism and Conservation: Manatees attract millions of visitors to Florida each year, supporting local economies and raising awareness about marine conservation. This economic value helps fund habitat protection, research programs, and education efforts that benefit many species beyond manatees.

Seed Spreaders: While manatees mainly eat leaves and stems, they occasionally consume seeds that pass through their digestive systems. As they travel and deposit waste, they help spread aquatic plants to new areas, supporting plant diversity throughout their range.

Water Quality Maintenance: By consuming large quantities of vegetation, manatees help prevent overgrowth that could choke waterways and reduce oxygen levels. Their grazing plays a vital role in keeping shallow coastal zones clean and balanced.

Natural Challenges

Adult manatees face remarkably few natural threats due to their large size, gentle habitat preferences, and the warm, shallow waters they call home. However, they do encounter some natural challenges that test their survival skills and adaptability.

Cold Stress: The greatest natural challenge for manatees is cold water. These tropical animals cannot survive extended exposure to temperatures below 60°F (15°C). When it gets too cold, manatees may suffer from "cold stress syndrome," which weakens their immune systems and leaves them vulnerable to infections like pneumonia. This is why they rely so heavily on warm-water refuges during winter months.

Predators for Young: Adult manatees have virtually no natural predators, but calves can occasionally be threatened by large sharks, American alligators, or crocodiles—especially where freshwater meets saltwater.

DID YOU KNOW?
- Manatees can suffer from frostbite! Even a brief dip into cold water can cause tissue damage and life-threatening stress.
- Hurricanes have stranded manatees miles inland when storm surges push them into flooded neighborhoods—sometimes leaving them stuck in backyards or drainage ditches!

Weather Extremes: Hurricanes and strong storms can create hazardous conditions for manatees. Powerful currents might separate calves from their mothers, storm debris can cause injury, and storm surges may strand manatees in unfamiliar or dangerous places when water recedes.

Disease and Parasites: Manatees can suffer from respiratory infections, skin conditions, internal parasites, and bacterial diseases. Their slow metabolism and relatively low body temperature can make it difficult for them to fight off infections quickly, especially when already stressed by cold water or poor nutrition.

Red Tide: Natural algae blooms, known as red tide, produce toxins that can harm or even kill manatees. They may inhale toxic air while surfacing or eat contaminated seagrass, leading to poisoning during red tide events.

Food Scarcity: Droughts, pollution, and natural events can damage or destroy seagrass beds, reducing food availability. In these situations, manatees must travel farther to find food or eat less nutritious alternatives.

Despite these natural challenges, manatees have developed strong survival strategies. Their long-distance travel skills, sensitivity to temperature, and the social knowledge passed between generations help them adapt to changing conditions in their aquatic world.

Human-Related Threats

While manatees have adapted well to natural challenges over millions of years, they face serious new threats from human activities in their increasingly busy aquatic neighborhoods. These slow-moving, trusting animals are particularly vulnerable because of their surface-breathing needs and curious nature.

Boat Strikes: Boat collisions are the leading cause of manatee injuries and deaths. Because manatees rest and breathe in shallow water, they are often hit by fast-moving boats. Many show permanent scars from propellers.

Habitat Destruction: Development along coastlines removes the seagrass beds, springs, and calm waters manatees need. Losing even one warm-water site can affect hundreds of animals.

Water Pollution: Polluted runoff and chemicals poison the water and the plants manatees eat. Algae blooms caused by fertilizers can kill seagrass and reduce oxygen in the water.

Entanglement: Fishing lines, nets, crab trap ropes, and other marine debris can wrap around manatees' flippers, tails, or necks. These entanglements can cut into their skin, restrict movement, interfere with feeding, or even cause drowning if they become anchored underwater.

Human Harassment: Despite being illegal under federal law, some people still attempt to swim with, touch, feed, or even ride wild manatees. These actions cause stress, alter their natural behavior, and may make them more likely to approach boats or humans in dangerous situations.

How You Can Help Manatee

- **Slow Down in Manatee Zones:** Obey speed limits in coastal areas.
- **Keep Your Distance:** Never touch, chase, or feed wild manatees.
- **Use Eco-Friendly Products:** Choose natural fertilizers and cleaners.
- **Support Conservation Efforts:** Donate to rescue and research groups.

Climate Change: Rising seas and unpredictable temperatures affect manatee habitats and food supplies. Some warm refuges may no longer stay warm enough.

Noise Pollution: Boats and coastal construction create underwater noise that confuses manatees and adds stress, interfering with their communication and navigation.

Life Span and Population

Manatees are remarkably long-lived animals with inspiring population recovery stories. In the wild, these animals typically live 50 to 60 years, though some individuals may reach 70 years or more. The oldest known captive manatee lived to age 69!

In the early 1970s, there were fewer than 1,000 Florida manatees left—a dangerously low number. Thanks to decades of protection, conservation, and education efforts, that number grew steadily. By 2016, the population reached over 6,600 and was downlisted from "endangered" to "threatened."

Recent Challenges: Since 2021, Florida manatees have faced an "Unusual Mortality Event," with over 1,000 deaths linked to seagrass loss and starvation in the Indian River Lagoon. The crisis revealed how quickly environmental changes can affect even recovering populations.

DID YOU KNOW?

- Scientists identify manatees by their scar patterns and track them through photo IDs taken during winter aerial surveys.

- A female manatee may give birth to only 5 or 6 calves in her entire lifetime due to their slow reproductive cycle.

Today, the Florida manatee population is estimated at 5,000 to 8,000. Exact counts are difficult due to constant movement between water bodies.

Global Populations: Other manatee populations face even greater threats:

- **Antillean manatees:** About 2,500 individuals spread across the Caribbean.
- **Amazonian manatees:** Roughly 10,000, but threatened by habitat loss and hunting.
- **West African manatees:** The most endangered, with fewer than 10,000.

Manatees reproduce slowly—females don't mature until age 4 to 6 and typically have just one calf every 3 to 5 years.

Manatees are far more than peaceful sea cows drifting through the water—they're living reminders of how delicate and resilient nature can be. These gentle giants have roamed tropical waters for millions of years, perfectly adapted to life in warm, shallow habitats. With their paddle-like flippers, temperature-sensing abilities, and unique underwater grazing skills, manatees fill an essential role as caretakers of coastal ecosystems.

They also teach us something deeper: that strength can be quiet, and progress can be slow but powerful. Manatees don't race, roar, or fight—but they thrive through gentleness, patience, and cooperation. They model what it means to live in harmony with others and with the natural world.

The dramatic recovery of Florida's manatee population—from just a few hundred individuals in the 1970s to thousands today—proves that conservation works. Laws, habitat protection, rescue efforts, and public education have made a meaningful difference. But recent events like widespread seagrass die-offs serve as urgent reminders that protecting manatees is an ongoing responsibility. Clean water, safe habitats, and climate action are more important than ever.

Manatees also inspire joy. They attract visitors, spark curiosity in young minds, and remind us that the ocean is full of wonder worth protecting. Their survival is tied to our choices—to slow down, respect nature, and support the efforts that keep our waters healthy.

By protecting manatees, we're also protecting everything they depend on and everything that depends on them—from seagrass and spring water to fish nurseries and coral reefs. Their story is not just about one species, but about the power of human action to repair and restore the planet.

As we look ahead, may the manatee continue to glide peacefully through our waters, not only as a symbol of conservation success, but as a call to action for the future of wildlife, water, and all who share this world.

Word Search

```
Y G B M X E M I G R A T I O N
H Z S C F F K E Z A R G O O O
A S F T H E E S H H A H U C D
I N L R S N T C D A E X U V Y
N O A O E I H G O Q B N P E U
E I C P A R E F D S O I E X F
R T G I C A R L L I Y T T G V
I A E C O M B C T I A S L A R
S T N A W P I A J N P V T T T
D P T L B T V E A C S P J E U
W A L A A R O M F J E D E D M
C D E U E T R E V B S O G R T
V A Q S T W E Q Y N A M W U S
T A N G W Q H S E A G R A S S
Y O D C X L A G O O N E S D I
C S L A M M A M V U J H A Y N
M X T G R H R E T A W M R A W
J F Q A D I R O L F G S P S V
```

Adaptations	Gentle	Marine
Aquatic	Graze	Migration
Calf	Habitat	Sea Cow
Conservation	Herbivore	Seagrass
Ecosystem	Lagoon	Sirenia
Flippers	Mammals	Tropical
Florida	Manatee	Warm Water

Resources and References

Bengston, J.L. Manatees and Dugongs: Status Survey and Conservation Action Plan. IUCN Species Specialist Group, 2002.

"Florida Manatee." Florida Fish and Wildlife Conservation Commission, 2024, https://myfwc.com/wildlifehabitats/profiles/marine/manatee/.

"Florida Manatee." Smithsonian's National Zoo and Conservation Biology Institute, 2024, https://nationalzoo.si.edu/animals/florida-manatee.

Hartman, Daniel S. Ecology and Behavior of the Manatee (Trichechus manatus) in Florida. American Society of Mammalogists, 1979.

"Manatee Research Program." Florida Atlantic University Harbor Branch Oceanographic Institute, 2024.

"Manatees." Save the Manatee Club, 2024, https://savethemanatee.org.

"Marine Mammal Protection Act." National Marine Fisheries Service, 2024.

Powell, James A. The Distribution and Biology of the West Indian Manatee. U.S. Fish and Wildlife Service, 1981.

Reynolds, John E., and Daniel K. Odell. Manatees and Dugongs. Facts on File, 1991.

"West Indian Manatee." U.S. Fish and Wildlife Service, 2024, https://www.fws.gov/species/west-indian-manatee-trichechus-manatus.

Published by Dylanna Press an imprint of Dylanna Publishing, Inc.
Copyright © 2025 by Dylanna Press
Author: Tyler Grady
All rights reserved. No part of this publication may be reproduced, stored in a retrieval system, or transmitted by any means, including electronic, mechanical, photocopying, or otherwise, without prior written permission of the publisher.

Although the publisher has taken all reasonable care in the preparation of this book, we make no warranty about the accuracy or completeness of its content and, to the maximum extent permitted, disclaim all liability arising from its use.